About Little Charlie Lindbergh

and other poems

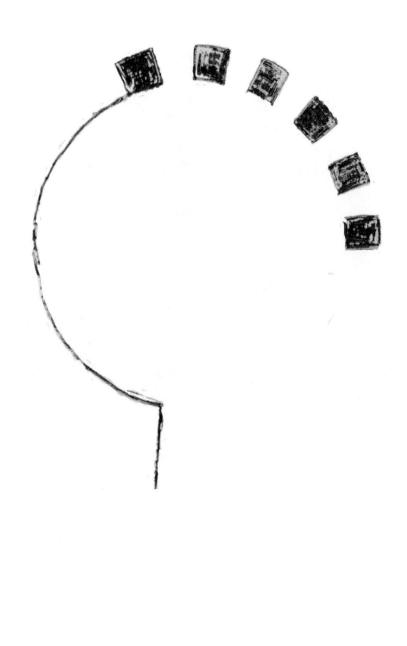

About Little
Charlie Lindbergh

and other poems

Margaret Randall

WingsPress

San Antonio, Texas
2014

About Little Charlie Lindbergh and other poems
© 2014 by Wings Press, for Margaret Randall.

Cover photograph, stone sculpture (theatre mask) from the amphitheatre
at Myra, Lycia (modern Turkey) © 2014 by Margaret Randall

Interior "vignette" drawings by Barbara Byers.

First Wings Press Edition

ISBN: 978-1-60940-403-1 (paperback original)
Ebooks:
epub ISBN: 978-1-60940-404-8
Kindle/mobipocket ISBN: 978-1-60940-405-5
Library PDF ISBN: 978-1-60940-406-2

Wings Press
627 E. Guenther
San Antonio, Texas 78210
Phone/fax: (210) 271-7805
On-line catalogue and ordering:www.wingspress.com
All Wings Press titles are distributed to the trade by
Independent Publishers Group
www.ipgbook.com

Library of Congress Cataloging-in-Publication Data

Randall, Margaret, 1936-
  [Poems. Selections]
  About little Charlie Lindbergh and other poems / Margaret Randall. --
First Wings Press edition.
    pages ; cm
  ISBN 978-1-60940-403-1 (pbk. : alk. paper) -- ISBN 978-1-60940-404-8
(epub ebook) -- ISBN 978-1-60940-405-5 (mobipocket ebook) -- ISBN
978-1-60940-406-2 (pdf ebook)
  1. Poetry -- American -- Historical analysis. I. Title.
  PS3535.A56277A6 2014
  811'.54--dc23
                                              2014007529

Contents

This book is for my partner Barbara,
my children Gregory, Sarah, Ximena and Ana,
and my grandchildren Lía Margarita, Martín, Daniel,
Richi, Sebastián, Juan, Luis, Mariana, Eli and Tolo.
A legacy in words.

About Little Charlie Lindbergh

and other poems

Because cosmic cyclical time finds it origins in the end and its end in the beginning, the ancient formula of the Andean Aymara is "the future to be found in the past." This concept of time and existence is so powerful that their verbs have no future tense.

—Stéfano Varese[1]

What would happen if one woman told the truth about her life? The world would split open.

—Muriel Rukeyser[2]

Preface

Nineteen-thirty-six. I hurried as always
but was late. Eight centuries
or ten thousand years,
my small story fixed to my back.
Food came weighed and wrapped,
shelter engorged as surplus.

My own, my own, my own
was a mantra I could sing
in any season.
I could be who I was
and also anyone else.

I was late and also much too early,
came to justice
before its time.
Unprepared to receive me,
its rough grasp hurt my hand,
embedded its promises in my flesh.

Juggling gender
I was early and also late.
Juggling children, service,
my explosion of words
on stone, parchment,
or floating cyber cloud.

Only poetry and love met me
where we laughed.
After so many false starts
they came in whole and sure
before the finish line.

My hand fit the ancient print,
a radius of living settled
on my shoulders.
I am lunar standstill now,
calendar of hope.

It is 2014, and I discover
I am perfectly on time.
Soon I will disappear
together with all my kind,
and the earth
with its synchronized clock
will wake some blue-green morning
its rhythms safe for a while.

For Every Two Steps Forward

Irony and unassuming wit
paint my everyday mask.
A question mark
where the mouth should be
adorns another.
A mask of kindness
always works
when promise comes up ominous.

I have fashioned these masks
through a lifetime of fear
and certainty, a step back
for every two steps forward.

I cannot remember
when the last mask dissolved
in a moment of blinding silence.
Touching raw skin still surprises.

Everyone Lied

We wanted to make the world a better place
but everyone lied,
fought power with humble flesh,
blood, brilliance,
and the luck of the innocent.

The enemy's lies assaulted us, their language
diminished our numbers,
turned us against one another,
touched lovers, confused our sense
of who we were and why.

And we lied about them, claimed they were
drug dealers and murderers,
all their food poisoned,
all their streets unsafe.
Then we lied about our own,
sowed serious doubt, set fatal traps.

Of course we lied to the CIA
and others who tortured us,
but also to our parents, children,
and those who came to us
for truth.

We lied by omission, convinced we must
reveal no contradiction.
The real story could only benefit
those who would destroy the dream,
who wanted us dead.
Accounts to be settled later.

We lied to protect our own and then
to justify not protecting our own.
We lied on a need to know basis,
parroted our leaders
even when they pretended genocide away.

We failed to question his disappearance,
100 knife-wounds in her body,
followed our leaders who lied to us,
then lied to ourselves:
the pain that changed our molecules.

Until later turned out to be the promise
we could not keep, a tired ghost
destined to wander hollow-eyed:
the lie that would come back to haunt
a sacrifice too big to name.

Things 1

Two drank from this vessel's duel spouts
ten thousand seasons past.
Lovers? Accused and accuser? Mother and child?

Small desert spiral might have signed
a spring or waterhole
or marked a supernova sighting.

Axe handle slept
in the Olduvai Gorge
until Leaky lifted it from sand.

Bronze Minoan bull startles time
as the small human figure
leaps again and again between its horns.

Iraqi clay tablet offers its story
of bureaucracy and beer
while the great Rosetta Stone

transforms Egyptian tax concessions
into verse, tedious
and thrilling simultaneously.

On a silver goblet hammered in Palestine
before the Christian doom
men and adolescent boys

come together in sexual ecstasy.
Pornography, mentoring
or simply love?

An Olmec mask floats
at the edge of dream,
its convex shape still warm

from the press of ancestral flesh,
faintly pocked and scarred
by *la cultura madre*.

Twenty-first century technology
lifts a ceramic fingerprint
left six thousand years before.

Teeth that cleaned a husk of kernels
deep in the Escalante
molder now, their energy spent.

These things that are more
than things
are messages waiting for us to turn and see,

objects and places witnessing
our need to know
how we descended from the trees.

Things 2

This spiral incised on a rock wall,
ancient feet in the Wadi Rum
and a pair with six toes each
staring back
from deep in Utah's canyons.

Clay, terracotta, bronze, papyrus,
or still-pungent gum
of Egyptian craft
ask questions of alabaster
in a Saharan cave.

Each carefully formed letter or glyph
clothes itself in come-on layers,
begs discovery
or cherishes anonymity.
Courage alone is translation.

How They Grab Our Words

He sent his water boy to spin the evidence:
weapons of mass destruction aimed at us.

When no WMD were found, he said:
Not sorry. The world's a better place.

Judged necessary sacrifice; 4,486 US soldiers dead.
A million Iraqis: collateral damage after all.

They used to ask: *What were you wearing?*
Now they declare *Boys will be boys.*

Do animals think? Do the disappearing glaciers
mean anything at all? Is up finally down?

Five years out of office, for the first time
the bully president gains a positive image.

They say we always like our presidents more
when they're no longer president.

It's all about the way they grab our words
and run, the end zone solidly in sight.

My Country

At this hour of winter north my country uncurls from sleep.
She moves in and out of a dream
where the Southern Cross plays close to the horizon.
That configuration of stars caresses her thighs
while keeping close their fading light.
My country is grumpy, reluctant to greet another day.

Storms assail one arthritic shoulder, monster storms
mythic before the moment of catastrophe.
Purposefully garbled language screeches in her ears.
She tries to repel the din, wipe rheumy sorrow
from the corners of her eyes, lure memory
and banish the ghosts that linger in her stiffened joints.

As sun warms, she covers her ears against a chorus
defying reflection, sworn enemies,
each out-shouting the other, each long ago
having forgotten that small kernel of meaning:
pure knowledge and intention of youth.
Exhaustion threatens. Only belligerence remains.

She tries to remember red stone buttes, Appalachian harmonies,
Harlem blues, the buffalo and a railroad to freedom.
She calls out to Crazy Horse[3] and Harriet,[4] Monk,[5] Adrienne,[6]
Popé[7] and that secret place off-limits to all perpetrators.
Every woman and man
who ever stood against the tide.

My country shivers where she lingers bedside,
knob-kneed, soles seeking purchase
on the cold planks of this new day.
Alone and burning with fever, she discovers
they have stolen her dignity,
the thousand masks she wore with joyful pride.

My country falls back to bed aware the virus is fatal.
She tries to conserve the strength
she knows she may still need,
searches for a writing instrument
and something on which to scribble
a few sure words no one may ever read.

Freedom They Make Sure

It was long ago and I was young but remember
the news of Bobby Sands' starvation death,
how the Irish Republican fought for visits and mail
and to be allowed to wear his own clothes,
how he refused to eat
and each day faded into the next day's dawn.

Those dusks and dawns clenched in tight embrace
and although they elected him to parliament
he died a prisoner on day 66.
Then, one after another, nine more prisoners
took his place, each dying in turn
until they threw an empire from its axis.

One prisoner after another spoke resistance
with the only weapon he had.
Those Irish freedom fighters rise in my eyes
as I listen to news from Guantánamo:
prisoners of 9/11, more than a decade
without trial or release.

One worked as a driver, another was 13
when captured and taken
to the other side of the world.
One weighs 77 pounds and we know
it is only a matter of time.
Like their Irish forebears

these men from nations that rankle our fear
are using their bodies,
what they have left
that is theirs, all theirs
to win a freedom they know
they will not live to see.

Place Cannot Betray

Right here at these death camps
time coaxes
to tourist destinations,
air still hisses poison gas
and moans of the dying echo.

In the crisp air of a high altitude path
families still sing *Guatemala,
no me abandonas*
a mile or two ahead of pursuing troops.

Night on Sudan's desert still holds
the tired feet
of children who believe
somewhere else exists.

Right here between the bedroom door
and eyes that fully know:
he is going to kill me now,
a burst of blood forever stains
this well polished floor.

A child's mouth screams
in a woman's face
the words she could not tell him then.
Place will not betray its evidence.

Shut Up, He Said

Shut up, he said. Then said it again.
Wittgenstein or the guy next door.
Rebel or president. Pious. Heroic.
Even the first time
I knew he meant more than *don't speak*.

Shut up, the torturer said, and you knew
he meant talk. Give me names.
Betray integrity. Save yourself.
Join the team that drags your loved ones
down in death.

Entitlement like a foul tobacco stream
or benevolent disguise.
I smother my voice
to ignite his power.
Our masks front silence

or perennial fear, pain, trauma,
an undoing so deep
and permanent
it scrubs both skin and memory
raw.

Power and control: gelatinous armature
topple building blocks

skewered together
with the bones of our wrists:
shattered each time we hold out our hands.

Silence of secrets, secret silence
where half a century later
women still won't speak
about the rape they endured,
the rape they waited for.

Silent nation where generations
still proclaim
an alternate story,
fashion the emperors' new clothes
while shivering in sorrowful rags.

Now a different silence touches my shoulder,
multicolor flames
beckon orange to blue and green,
seduce from beyond a broken border
draw me into ambiguous embrace.

Chosen silence reaches for my throat,
usurps the word *home*
even when its letters startle
this voice I've honed 77 years
against such heritage of denial.

This new *don't speak* avoids the ugly detour:
sound of raindrops, clang of prison door,
wind's husky voice,
water not meant to cleanse but kill,
a lie that stands where truth gave up the fight.

Would silence as exercise
—my decision now—
be addition or subtraction,
welcome gift
or cowering emptiness?

If I pose the challenge in questions:
could I last a day?
What bridge would take me
to my final resting place:
language of my invention?

Beside My Bed

At three or four I woke uncurling child's fists,
to touch the smooth satin binding
of my peach-colored blanket.
Holding tight I counted to seven
so my closet door wouldn't open
to reveal its dark ceiling aperture,
attic of evildoers waiting to attack.

In my twenties I emerged from sleep
to finger a pack of L & M's,
reached for first cigarette of the day,
lit and inhaled the habit
that forty years later
would cancel my breath,
bring sorry pause.

Now I wake, reach out and you are here:
warm from sleep,
sweet in long love.
If I extend my other hand to bedside table
I touch only trifocals on spindly stems
and a nautilus shell,
its golden stripes singing ocean camouflage.

Joining of No Return

Where rock meets rock along the jagged cleft
above Pueblo Bonito's back wall,
where brick floats upon mythic emptiness
in Hagia Sofia's great dome,
where calligraphy becomes art
when image is forbidden above the entranceway
to an abandoned *caravansarai*
and the Silk Road sorts its memories,
there is a joining of no return.

Nothing messy about these seams,
nothing left over.
A waning sun turns the Nile's expanding ripples
to brief ridges of copper light
as sun turns wave fields on the Mekong,
Irrawaddy or Colorado the same haunting hue.
Yet all waves belong only to themselves
and along the lines where each river laps its shore
a line separates seeing from unknowing.

Such borders drip salt on slightly parted lips,
images embed themselves
in age-mottled flesh.
Great stones placed by the Inca
in perfect harmony
issue words I feared I might forget.

Each migration held by invisible mortar
imprints itself upon this landscape
unfolding on my tongue.

Where your skin and mine knit tight
between your right breast
and my left,
our bodies fit together perfectly,
and despite our sudden hot-flash blooms
touch speaks its language of years.
Here every cell brings memory home,
every nerve ending rests
at the boundary along which we grow.

Tipping Point

*Written after a deranged youth
entered an elementary school
in Newtown, Connecticut
on December 14, 2012,
killing 20 children and 6 staff.*

Their teachers pass out crayons,
tell stories to calm their fear,
are willing to die
trying to save them
and die beside them instead.

A hundred thousand paper snowflakes
infuse their town with solace.
A president comes to console.
Briefly
a national dialog begins.

No stories or crayons, no snowflakes
or national conversation
for Chicago's children:
just as tender but black or brown
and poor,
murdered each night by violence
unremarkable in ghetto land.

Every South Side street
cradles the body
of some mother's son,

some kid who might still have time
before answering the call
to greater madness.

Bullets pierce air and walls
and the heads of youngsters
who might have grown
to be teachers or doctors
or been forced
to march to patriotic war.

And from such war
each evening's news
brings stories
of drone attacks
where weddings looked like
terrorist training camps
or schools were mistaken for convoys.

We mute the sound, fearing
the tipping point
may ruin our dinner.
A tipping point is a curious thing
as it settles between the left
and right sides of the brain.

When the pendulum returns
to its indifferent center
and we return to life as usual
we forget there was
a tipping point at all.

Personal Cartography

I couldn't stay away, not forever, although
spring winds parched my throat
and tiny cactus needles
pierced the flesh of my breasts.

Three hundred sixty degrees of cloudless sky
spun my head until graying eyes
threatened to jump
orbits unable to rein them in.

Then a furious thunderhead
released its ferocity
of desert storm,
scouring life from canyon walls.

Towering red rock fortresses
pressed in on either side,
wringing awe
from stooped shoulders.

Silky wax of the single bloom
on a defiant Prickly Pear
met my fingertips,
reminding me survival matters.

The Poets Are Leaving

The poets are leaving, those I knew growing up
who shared my decades and discoveries,
gave voice to my generation's need.

Losing Adrienne[8] when her lifetime of pain
overpowered that singular voice,
clarity of being turned clarity of speech.

Losing Grace,[9] her small compact body
packing one last revelation
behind the stories that define our lives.

And losing Anselm,[10] bright blue eyes twinkling
in Finnish, French, German, English,
traveling boots ready at the foot of his bed.

Some couldn't bear another dead child, war, or lie
contrived to shelter wholesale greed.
Some, because human, had more personal reasons.

Some fought their unexpected marching orders
with every verb in their arsenal.
Some went easily, sure they'd left their mark.

Some losses, like Gloria[11] who redrew borders
or Meridel[12] who reshaped territories of allegiance:
difficult to mend the fabric they left undone.

Some, like Langston,[13] Gwendolyn,[14] Allen[15] or Creeley,[16]
left echoes we still hear
in the voices we give birth to.

They have taken their places beside Whitman[17] and H.D.,[18]
Rukeyser[19] and Williams,[20] in the great American idiom:
a chorus deafening in righteous dissonance.

We don't lack for new poets hip-hopping, slamming
or performing on the page, their voices
enticing us with promises of what's to come.

But the departed poets have left an emptiness
impossible to fill. If I believed in an afterlife
I might imagine a marathon reading

in perfect pitch, dissonant silence, disembodied voices
sounding in multidimensional harmony
to a grateful public: poetry-lovers all.

I Do Not Bow My Head

I do not bow my head. Maybe years ago
but these days
when someone commands
let us bow our heads or *observe a moment of silence*
and all chins drop and eyes lower,
I hold mine high,
unwilling to honor the fictitious power.

Celebrate, yes. Submit, no.
Sometimes I close my eyes,
no gesture of reverence but journey
inward to my core.
I do not deny
the deep place others hold in me
or refuse tribute to children or mentors,
those connections that have made me strong.

I do not deny my smallness either
or pretend I am anything
more than one aging woman
born almost eight decades ago
straddling centuries and questions.
Slowly, over that minute or two
I straighten my shoulders,
refuse to bend my knees
in humbled posture.

Instead, I lift my chin, stand tall,
sure there is nothing and no one
up there, out there, anywhere
but here
in this fierce energy
I rouse and tame by turn.

Tired of Writing from This Bent Body

Tired of writing from this bent body,
tissue-thin skin and bookish mind,
for one long night
I want to exhale the breath of that woman
sitting on Aztec stone, Mexican market 1962.

I want to hold her hunger and chapped hands
arrange the *rebozo's* frayed edge
about her infant's cheek, also chapped and red
despite soiled cloth and gaunt heat
of its mother's breath.

I want to open my mouth and speak Pashto or Dari
muffled behind the heavy folds of dark cloth
revealing only my eyes
attentive to a world beyond my reach:
not imagined but looked upon full face.

I want the strength inside Malala's target head
not on the world stage but long before
in a hospital bed beneath bone shards and pain,
fear slowly taking her
where she was meant to be.

For one day I would like to speak the Mandarin
of fresh flowers Ai Weiwei places

each morning in a bicycle basket
outside his gate,
the artist's protest of freedom denied.

Daughter of Hue, my tonality has perfect pitch.
Xosa clicks at the back of my throat
while Arabic and revenge pound my video recording,
Father Son and Holy Ghost,
intoned by the believer I cannot be.

I want to make poetry in another's tongue
with reflected glow, not fluorescent beam
as tribal child or child of my city
born into the wrong family, body, sensibility,
terror devouring my spine.

I want to release the call of migrating wildebeests
running the Serengeti with their zebra friends,
translate Coyote's high-pitched wail
or song of a single canyon wren
shattering dawn's busy quiet.

I want to be each of them and others
long enough to remember
what they remember,
tell their stories from identity out
but here I stand: irremediably other,

monolingual, unique, myself.

With Gratitude to Vallejo

One day, it will be my turn. Luck of the draw
even for me.
One day, almost certainly not in Paris,
a chance in seven on a Thursday,
the door that burst open on December 6, 1936
will close.

It will slam shut or settle like velvet
until its light dims completely,
the rhythms of its tongue gone still.

My turn, not because I have tied my wrist bones
on wrong,
braided anxious fingers,
stumbled into the abyss
or laughed when I might have cried.

I breathed available air,
loved in every way I knew
followed my map to a place beyond canyon walls.

After the door
swung open between my mother's thighs
and before my turn's arrival
my children and their children will reach
for places I cannot know
while I am warmed

by a love that dares speak its name,
black words on white pages,
this nest woven of numbers and sky.

Like Making Soup

It would be smoky if any of us still smoked.
Those days long gone to years
and without the smoke
it's a daze born of melted feeling
wrapping its arms about midnight.

What we know without taking notes,
without stopping to rationalize
today's synaptic connections.
There's just so much you can learn,
then it stops.

It's like making soup. Without thinking
you choose a few
well-matched ingredients,
this and that.
No system to limit the imagination.

More an end count of combinations
found on Fulton Street at 4 a.m.,
Mexico's *La Merced*,
or the old Cuban ration book.
A coming together of senses.

This mind-soup depends on numbers
and letters, whole words

seven thousand years in the making
skipping from stone to stone
as it crosses a stream of consequence.

Pick an image from the pile, bring it
close to your myopic eyes.
A jazz trill helps you settle back,
sink into your seat
and let memory's experience wander.

Without Warning

At the bus stop and out of the corner of my eye
I see myself waiting,
awkward bundle at my feet.
I am wearing the same sky blue fleece
though it hangs looser against my body.
My hair, still long and full and brown,
frames the younger me in her oblivion.

I swerve and almost hit the car to my right,
snap my neck
to get one last glimpse of myself
before people I loved
took what wasn't theirs,
a child stopped calling home,
and temperature threatened my planet.

Without warning I make a U-turn
and slow way down
to observe every detail
of my younger self.
I even consider a shouted question
might bring an answer
against all mathematical odds.

She looks straight at me and smiles.
I smile back
and keep on driving,
hoping to keep
my appointment with myself.

Da Vinci's Proportions

Anti-Vitruvian, we revel
in the messy leftovers
after Leonardo's circle and square
conquer millennial thinking.

When life is no longer made
to fit well-oiled principles,
all maps can be redrawn,
all joys are possible.

Pressed Into Dubious Service

Something huge is in the air.
It is World,
immense yet unseen—
brushing cheek or consciousness.

I walk up, extend fingers,
then the flat of a palm,
want to touch this thing
that tugs as it evades.

Rouault's thick black lines
caress a map
holding the residue of love
in radiant explosion.

We know a presence of danger,
Ground Zero metaphysics
pressed into dubious service:
words changing places with words.

Pain: does it belong to history
or me alone?
Is this the perfect storm
or a lonely sign?

I walk as tall as I can
around the road's final bend
hoping for answer
but finding only questions.

About Little Charlie Lindbergh

The truth about little Charlie Lindbergh's
murder,
A hero's dark love of eugenics,
President Kennedy's lone killer,
or the Tonkin Gulf incident?
Ghosts that still haunt us
pushing fantasy as fact
or fact as fantasy.

A year before I was born, Mother
gave birth to her first daughter,
named Margaret
and dead within hours.
I too am Margaret.
She always said she was pregnant
with me eighteen months.

Throughout her long life
she repeated
that other Margaret's name
and the story of her birth and death
until once, toward the end,
she turned to me in mock surprise
and asked
How could you think such a thing?
You have the wildest imagination!

A gesture here, comment there,
years of disparate clues
slipped between my anxious fingers
or lodged themselves in doubt.
The twin name unraveled,
mysterious death remained.

Facts erased in a moment,
then reinforced:
Mother's fear of illness—
the common cold
but also quieter hidden ills,
unseen and menacing.

Pressing my brother
not to date
the college sweetheart
whose sister was rumored
to be mentally ill.
Fear of the raucous gene
compounding a shadowy blight.

I'd point out the mental illness
rife in our family as in many.
For Mother,
if no one saw
it wasn't there.

Grandfather just a dreamy old man.
Grandma's biting petulance,
her lies.

Uncle took a drink too many
but wasn't an alcoholic.
Never giving in to his gay identity:
all of it choice, not tragedy.

No wooden ladder remains standing
against the open second-story window
of a New Jersey mansion
in my family history.

No grassy knoll
obscures another script.
No fabricated strike
authorized a war
that would claim two million lives
and usher in the right to first attack.

My family secrets were humbler,
easier to hide.
They shaped individual
rather than collective lies.
They only made me crazy,
didn't seed posttraumatic stress
among nations.

Trumping the Storyline

Two hundred eighty thousand years ago
in today's Ethiopia
a Stone Age genius
fashioned obsidian into a perfect weapon,
fitted it to a strong shaft
and speared what we imagine
as community dinner.

The discovery astounds, yet I wait
for the wall beyond daily use
that filled our ancestors' eyes
with held breath,
explosion of stars at high noon,
the gentlest caress
of memory hurtling centuries.

Unfolding or unwinding from brains
we judge lesser because smaller,
do hidden images still wait for us
in some lost cave obscured by time?
May we still be privy
to that dazzle of passion
spread like lightning before our eyes?

Homo heidelbergensis aka Heidelberg Man
was tall and muscular: a body type
not unlike our own.

Archeologists calculate a prehistoric
assembly line.
Beneficiaries of the new technology
threw from a distance but left no evidence

of who their victims were. Wooly Mammoth?
Giant Sloth? Legged-fish or a lonely band
of dinosaurs evading extinction?
We may speculate our species
older by millennia, rearrange
the branches on our family tree,
or add a talented predecessor,

but I keep waiting for evidence of art
that trumps the story line,
curls away from the need for food
or clothing, reaches sky
to grab rainbows
and weave their colors
into a fabric neither ingested nor worn.

Lips Long Since Returned to Forest Mulch

The Maya wrote their concept of zero
as a resting oval with small curved lines,
one on top, two at the bottom,
coming together in points at either end.
Three shorter lines
rise within like eyelashes or tiny sails.

The glyph is a leaf, a seed, an eye, but not only.
Something about the image escapes
when I approach,
hides in a region I will never see.
Imagination loses me
in canyons of mossy stone.

Hull and sails gone to mystery
in a place so inland from oceans
and outlier to deciphering minds
centuries before sailing vessels
crossed our horizons:
symbol of emptiness filled.

Pale blue washes my dream
and that glyph invites me
into its home.
I am both eager and afraid.
When I enter my skin glistens
with gold dust oblivious to market worth.

Expressing zero, the Maya didn't mean nothing,
an idea that baffled Europeans
as late as the Renaissance.
A void neither native to its vigesimal place
nor absence
waiting for something to happen.

Like the dot representing one
or bar claiming five,
this small basket boat had its work cut out
along the Long Count
or Calendar Round:
endless legacies of birth and death.

In my dream there is always someone
I know well
and someone I meet for the first time.
Familiarity and fear
shoot their arrows
into the six regions of my heart.

They etch themselves on my skin like Nazi numbers
or tracer flares from dictates
claiming to comfort
those taught to believe that wars end war,
our love is unnatural, learning isn't for girls
or some humans prefer poverty.

I ask myself if mathematical brilliance
kept the Maya safe from storms,
coaxed crops or helped cacao beans
journey from tree to rich brown liquid

filling clay mugs
raised to lips long since returned to forest mulch.

We are drawn to examine a weighted base
and three flickers of hope.
I want to reach out and take this zero
between my fingers' broken feathers,
follow its burning light to questions
unanswered then and now.

Until we inhale the air they breathed
into our own lungs,
unless we can feel what they felt
walking toward the sacrificial bench,
the code may be broken and broken again
but will not let us in.

Pangaea

Pangaea wasn't the first supercontinent,
its C-shaped embrace
rising from seas we can no longer name.
Eons into earth's past Nuna broke apart
then reassembled as Rodinia.
Pannotia preceded the map we travel.

The poles played desperate games
with the equator.
Siberia danced with the Maghreb,
oceans yawned
then clenched their teeth
while Brazil rubbed shoulders with West Africa.

Rock magnetism and fossils hold proof
of tectonic wars, wild collisions,
ruptures that make child's play
of Himalaya's upward thrust,
Pompeii's last gasp or the mudslide
that erased forty Andean villages.

The breakup was slow but would have stopped
the sturdiest heart.
Until 1492 when a maligned adventurer
temporarily reknit Pangaea's seams,
sending tomatoes to Italy
and chili peppers to Thailand.

Oranges landed in south Florida
only to empower Anita Bryant
to vicious hate.
Global trade only as beautiful
as the justice it births,
the tenderness that laps its shores.

Posidonia Oceanica

Measuring human age, we are careful to guess
this side of obvious,
ignore stained teeth and scarred skin
or thinning hair,
focus on deflected light
in eyes begging us to lie.

Less sentient life has no such hope.
A patch of *Posidonia oceanica*,
species of sea grass called Neptune,
has just given up its DNA,
claiming at 200,000 years
the title of oldest living organism.

This hardy Mediterranean carpet
reproduces asexually, clones itself
through undersea meadows
from Spain to Cyprus.
One patch is 2,000 miles long
bobbing and waving its ancient flag.

Our odd love affair with biggest or oldest
burns our candle at both ends,
while those who contemplate
the single blade of grass
or stunning silence
explore less relevant regret.

The Language of Mountains

Twice shaking me like an open wound,
the sound of a mountain
parting at the seams.

Seated on Machu Picchu's low stone wall,
boulders so perfectly placed
I hear a one-note harmony.

Dulled in early morning mist, the roar
takes seconds to reach our ears:
rock gifting us its break with time.

Later in Grand Canyon's inner gorge,
small sounds of night creatures
vying with water's thunder as we sleep.

Sudden and distant along the river corridor
rock leaves rock,
scarring this landscape's Precambrian face.

Like the tree that falls where no one hears,
echo registers its confounding story:
memory's memory of itself.

When Drones Replace the *Enola Gay*

His name might be Carlos or Barry.
When his 12-hour shift is over
he comes home
and plays with the twins,
maybe listens to some 'trane,
speaks, makes love, sees friends.

That was before. Now he works
in a darkened room
and the Air Force
when it mentions his job
talks about the stress
of analyzing images in motion
hour after hour, year after year.

No windows and the room is clean.
If he asks himself the question
he hears himself repeat
democracy democracy
but the word has become a thin film
of ash beneath his nails,
clogging his pores
and he looks away
even when he wants your eyes.
One of the twins smiles crooked-lipped
like him.

He knows they shoot horses
if they break a leg
but his own veins burst
when the gate springs open
and he's way back on the track
the other horses off
and running fast, mud for glory
and all of them filled with a purpose
he cannot remember.

By displacement and distance
the monitor separates him
from that war on the ground,
promises a castle in the air
and draws a line in the sand
meant to save him from guilt and shame.

I say his name might be Carlos
but it's just my imaginary
trying to put a face to a number
invisible as the enemy
he's been taught is devious, deviant,
doesn't like 'trane or have
a wife and twins.

Despite the miles, invisibility
and blurred vision
guilt and shame creep in
and he needs psychologists
and chaplains 24/7
to help him survive
remote attack.

Headlines shout applause
when terrorists die
but silence the wedding party:
27 members of a single family,
11 kids out for recess,
every one a case of mistaken identity.

Carlos's children walk to school
on a quiet Midwestern street
but he dreams
of the guy with the oversize pack,
pressure cookers stuffed with dynamite,
biggest fireworks you can buy.

Maybe he's not Carlos but Andy,
his children Jeannie and Little Jeff.
His wife might be Beulah
or Aisha or Qui, turtle
in Vietnamese.

Since 9/11 drone intelligence is up
seven thousand percent.
Every day the unmanned planes
transmit 1,600 hours of video.
And *Gorgon Stare*,
like his boy's favorite video game,
scans cities in a single sweep.

When a rocket hits the only hospital
for two hundred miles
he repeats the story
he learned at orientation:

mistakes happen
and victims are likely sympathizers,
a dead terrorist one terrorist less.

For years he's stared at shadows
on a screen,
women walking to and from market,
scattered villages
where the appearance of newcomers
heats his appetite.

Then, shift done, he drives home,
face a twitching mask
of frightened skin.
He doesn't think about the twins,
only getting up tomorrow
and taking his seat again.

In this new generation of warfare
drones have replaced the *Enola Gay*
and Carlos's job
is to sit before a screen
where the unmanned plane
does its lethal job
without exposing him to harm.

Blood Trail

*Written after the April 24, 2013 Bengladesh
garment factory collapse in which 1,124 died
and approximately 2,500 were injured.*

Instant pressure from a photographer's finger
shows us the man's head bowed in death,
eyes closed and outstretched arms
embracing the woman beside him,
also dead.
We long to inhabit the moment
just before those deaths.

The bunched knot of the woman's sari
in pink and orange bloom
weeps through broken brick
and splintered wood.
Bits of twisted rebar,
a devastated beam
wrapped in a bolt of cloth gone mad.

That beam may have been the weapon
that pinned her to this rubble
of collapse.
More than a thousand were crushed
when the factory fell.
Our nightly news fills with rage
at easy building codes,
an owner who didn't care,

a country so far away
its pain never reaches us.

Always somewhere else.
I am afraid
to look at the label
on my latest purchase,
a breezy summer blouse
from Gap or Ralph Lauren,
afraid it will say *Made in Bangladesh*
or let loose a blood trail
no *Tide Ultra* can remove.

Shame

In the four regions of my heart
the tower's mad collapse
once again gives birth to languages
undecipherable for those
who grew up in city heat,
took refuge on rusted schoolyard swings
or downed egg creams at the corner candy store.

We were who we were, and every purposeful turn
toward poetry's invitation of tongues
meant opening a book
we might not have opened
or braving the trade winds
threatening to pull my major muscle
from familiar comfort.

Tricuspid risks tonalities
that sound beyond my ear.
Pulmonic takes an absent breath
and runs a marathon
of awkward legs.
Mitral shelters mystery
while *aortic* pumps new blood.

The trapeze artist almost misses
her partner's flying wrists
but grabs and holds.

In the stands
a wave of fearful thrill recedes,
leaving a beach
disabled by death's overdraw.

We close our eyes against images
we know won't leave us
in blind peace,
travel arteries like highways
crush fear beneath our feet.
A single word
unleashes waterfalls.

In dreams we pull up hard
before the wind-swept precipice,
explore what poetry is made of
when we've lived longer
than have left to live
and every word counts twice.
Shame is the cunning adversary,
language our salvation on the rise.

Juan's Triangles

for my grandson,
Juan Pérez Mondragón

You are all about triangles, Juan:
Bermuda, Golden
and the Triangle of Dragons.
A space of mystery
where things disappear
and come back differently.

Even continents. You have your theory
of what happened to that land mass
you're sure rests seven thousand feet
beneath ship-eating waves.
You bring news of three pyramids,
one entirely of glass.

All manner of maps unfold behind your eyes
and you want to know if this one
is wrong like Mercatur's, weighted north?
Or is it a good map like the Peters Projection
where continents and countries
hold their own?

Your eight years pulse insatiable motion
from Columbia to Pangaea
and eons into the future.

Your strong little arms
embrace tectonic clash.

A meteorite parts oceans
in your memory
and every year adds new rooms
to your imaginary's house.
But I take refuge in the old,

watch you unfurl the Tropic of Cancer
from earth's bloated waist,
grab its frayed end and swing
out   out
where my years follow
but cannot hold or tether you
to yesterday.

His Only Begotten Son

In 1510 or thereabouts
parents of the Mexican Isthmus
sold their ten-year-old daughter
into slavery.
In time she became a symbol of scorn:
she who slept with the enemy,
mother of a mongrel race.

Further south, in the silver mining city
of Potosí,
parents maimed their young sons
so they wouldn't have to labor
in the mercury pits.
A version of kindness
when considered in context.

In India, several centuries later,
when husbands died
child brides were buried alive.
Bound Chinese feet, Ottoman concubines,
conquest and slave auction:
children murdered by those
whose job it was to love and protect.

These children we birth
and say we love.
Distinguished fathers

in every country
raping their girls or
—depending on preference—
their boys.

For God so loved the world,
that he gave his only begotten Son,
that whosoever believeth in him
should not perish
but have everlasting life.[21]

Father, Son and Victim

After seeing "Hannah Arendt"

At the trial she watched an unrepentant man
in charge of transport, cattle cars
packed with those he sent to die.
A bureaucrat following orders.

He showed surprise, impatience
when the Court refused to understand
he was only doing his job:
chain of command, an orderly society.

She called it _the banality of evil_
and, a Jew herself,
reported on the treachery
of certain Jewish leaders.

Friends stopped being friends.
Even family didn't understand.
Colleagues tried to prevent her from teaching
but her students demanded her gift.

Hitler . . . Himmler . . . Eichmann.
Nixon . . . Abrams . . . Calley.
Cheney . . . Bush . . . Schwarzkopf.
Obama . . . Hagel . . . Allen.

Pope, cardinal, bishop and parish priest
like father, son and victim,
authority delivers pomposity of pain
while leaders shape such loyal following.

She taught us we cannot hide
in *them* and *us*,
but to fear the them in us,
to dig beneath convenient blame.

Older Than the Oldest

*Based on information in
Rabbi Herschel Schacter's
New York Times obituary,
March 26, 2013.*

Sixty-eight years before he died
a US Army rabbi
entered Buchenwald.
He would carry the sting of smoke
and smell of burning flesh
every minute of his long life.

What he saw shattered measure
that April 11th of 1945.
From beneath one pile of bodies
a brief gesture of movement
rose to meet his eyes.

He reached to steady prisoner 17030
and asked *How old are you?*
The child, whose name was Lulek,
whispered *What difference does it make?*
I am older than you, anyway.
You cry and laugh like a child,
I haven't laughed in a long time
and I don't cry anymore.

Other survivors begged to be told
if the world was aware
of what they'd endured.
Lulek never asked that question.

In his seven years he'd grown older
than the oldest among them.
He knew the world knew
and if the unspeakable
had been perpetrated against him
it would be perpetrated against others.

Sixes

A single roll of dice offers 36 chances
you'll get doubles,
while the Buddha fasted six years
only to find extreme asceticism
brought him no closer to enlightenment
than his earlier life of palace luxury.

The sixth amendment to our Constitution
calls for due process,
a fair and speedy trial by jury,
the right to confront one's accuser,
obtain witnesses,
retain counsel.

If you are Catholic or Lutheran
the Sixth Commandment
says you may not commit adultery
which, as we know,
may be interpreted in many ways
and is.

If you are Jewish, Greek Orthodox
or Protestant (except Lutheran)
the same Commandment says
you may not murder.

Some people consider adultery
worse than murder,
others take adultery, thank you.

Hindu Kali, she of the six arms,
is goddess of time, destruction
and death.
She is also associated
with sexuality and violence,
then again with motherly love.

When the five-color pie is not enough
a sixth color—purple—
arrives as the color of Zen,
shapeshifting or philosophy
of the immaterial. The color purple
is an alternate reality.

Six of one, half a dozen of the other
my mother used to say.
I never knew
if she wanted to ease my mind
no matter which I chose
or really thought it was the same.

All these affirmations
and each alone
may seem contradictory
until we understand
nothing is what it seems to be,
no system arrives or survives intact.

Photographic Memory

The photograph, reprinted so often it's engraved
upon a billion sets of eyes,
turns 50 years old today.
More accurately: 50 years and seconds,
the number of seconds it took those practiced smiles
to shatter as one shot then another
tore through a sunny Dallas morning
when the presidential motorcade
made its slow way past the Book Depository
then stopped forever in a nation's narrative.

Kennedy's hand appears to be coming up to wave,
Jackie's hair is licked by a gentle breeze
beneath her famous pillbox hat.
Governor Connally and his wife sit in front,
his frown and searching eyes perhaps
a premonition of the moment.
If King had not stepped out on that motel balcony,
if Mercader's raincoat hadn't hidden
the icepick that ended Trotsky's life,
if Benazir Bhutto hadn't raised her head

through the open top of her campaign vehicle
at just that moment,
history might have continued its course
instead of veering into the dark tunnel
of no return.

Yet there was no flash across a television screen
when a boardroom decision murdered a country
or I raged at my daughter
when her father pushed me to madness.

Such moments hide from public sight,
but like the child who dies of hunger
every ten seconds in this unjust world
or the lie that rallies us to kill,
loss climbs another flight of stairs
tripping over lives that might have been,
no rewind possible, no erasure
where time's spiral
demands first crimes first
before we sleep the night.

Tower of Babel

Chalky black felt moves silently
across my lips
erasing words
as if they were scrawled
upon a third grade blackboard.

Another word goes.
I dream its shape and weight
but cannot speak its name.
Will I run into it again?
Will it still belong to me?

I have not been able to follow
a map to the chamber
of wayward syllables,
that cavernous place
where Mandarin scales,

German philosophers' stones,
the click of Xosa tongue
or lilt of Spanish fairytale
threaten detours
before I reach my goal.

A tower of Babel crowds my mouth.
I am not greedy, don't crave
new language or unfamiliar sound.

Only those beloved words
I once cradled between my teeth.

Other Storylines

What screams from the window
of that car idling beside yours
cannot be described as sound,
music's history
stuffed deep in frayed pockets.

Aroused only by whip and chains
she claims she is in control.
All other storylines
whither in memory
or cower beneath the bed.

In the torture chamber
he is detached,
keeps his *right* and *wrong*
in clear perspective,
his prisoner an afterthought.

The suicide bomber straps
and buckles his bulky vest,
closes his eyes
and utters his last sad words:
I matter.

Through Mud of War and Muck of Promise

A fan of interlocking scenes
etched on the underbelly
of expectation:
third from left
has an ever-rising sun
and dependable climate.

I must reach to glimpse
farthest to right,
its mirage of answers
so far beyond their questions
the space between
swells in broken labyrinth.

Take all of me pleads my life,
still urging
holistic solution.
We are more than the sum
of paltry choices
available at birth.

Minutes dance to a beat
surprised
by unexpected quarter notes,
Harmony enters
only where something stolen
is replaced by risk.

We hurry to follow those tiny arrows
stitched to the underside
of eyelids
or along the heart's retaining wall
through mud of war
and muck of promise.

While the rhythm of lockstep
and resignation
holds out its cajoling hand
a new wind invites us
to make one last chance
our best.

Roses Tremble

The President is speaking
in the garden.
He says this might happen
or possibly that.
Roses tremble
from a deafening rumble

soaring in growing crescendo,
shattering the windows
of the First Secretary's office.
Her secretary
calls a press conference
but no one gets the message.

They are all busy monitoring
a meteor the size of Chicago
whose trajectory has earth
squarely in its cross-hairs.
Outer space
holds their attention

so no one hears the rumble
until the planet's center
implodes with a roar
that is only a shudder now,
destroying every small hope
and grandiose prophecy.

As If It Had No Teeth

No one is left to tend the garden
so we cannot be sure
if war is born
and dies with us
or the water your faucet gives
is killing you slowly.

The ferocity of a Midwest tornado
unleashes fire on mountain trees
brittle from the Bark Beetle's
last meal.
Manhattan Island floats away
in a rain of ten thousand days.

We cannot go gently
into a night
woven of denial and lies
arranged by shape and size:
insider trading
on the "down low."

I only hope someone is
keeping a record,
writing it all down,
and doesn't call it
prehistory
as if it had no teeth.

Up Through the Clouds

Purposeful, blindered, this
regiment of minutes
ticks along
behind my wary eyes.
They are my minutes
and only I see them.

When they come upon others
they quicken their step.
The arrow says *one way only*
and I fear
the tiny increments will obey
as long as they are able.

Only the softest shadow of regret
might cause them to stumble
and fall,
move backward in disarray
or climb up through the clouds
and disappear

like those buffalo in the
Barry Lopez story
witnessed by a party of Cheyenne
camped on the Laramie Plain
near the Medicine Bow Mountains,
winter of 1845.[22]

It is all about direction
and language:
the expertise of feet,
how one sound hides within another,
how nouns and verbs
spar or dance together.

People between two rivers
situate their adjectives
with care.
A female word
must run to catch up
with power's golden crown.

It takes the perfect storm of
happenstance and disbelief
brought together
by one too many lies
woven into the texture
of our lives.

It takes horror
disguised as life as usual.
Time's forward motion
stops, shifts,
leaves you peering at 1491
with a 2014 promise on your lips.

His Name was Emmett Till
His Name was Trayvon Martin[23]

His name was Emmett Till, fourteen,
—friends called him Bobo
because of his stutter—
down from Chicago
to the town of Money, Mississippi,
running in the delta with his cousins.

Double-bubble, please ma'am,
at the neighborhood grocer.
They said he whistled
at the pretty white woman,
already fancied himself a man.

The crackers who kidnapped,
beat and murdered him,
hung fifty pounds of steel
around his neck
before throwing him in the Tallahatchie,
never believing they'd do time.

Laughing into their spittoons,
boasting of their exploit
in every backwoods backroom bar,
sold their story to Look Magazine
for $4,000. Serious sport.

Fifty-eight years later,
George Zimmerman
didn't need a white robe
to hunt down Trayvon Martin
in the soft rain of Sanford, Florida.

The neighborhood watchman
defied police orders
to stay in his car,
took refuge in Stand Your Ground,
harassed the young man
until he had to defend himself,
then shot him at close range.

Emmett and Trayvon, so close
in age, both executed
by white vigilantes
who lust to murder black children
—no other way to say this—
and 58 years
haven't changed the equation.

Emmett, Trayvon, and all black children
in between
whose faces didn't make
the 5 o'clock news
but dared to believe
they had a right to live.

It's the little things
lodge in my heart:
Emmett's bubble gum,

the *Skittles* Trayvon
bought to share
while watching the game
he never got to see.

And those mysteries
we will never know:
the precise moment
light goes out
in the eyes of a dying child,
the intimate sound
his secrets make
as they splinter against the wall.

Children Still Run in Silence

Today I turned the last shovel
of warm Masaya earth.
I mean the last shovel
before hitting bone,
one more skull
dislodged from its body
by time's fictitious count.

Three decades have passed
but time stops and starts,
detours treachery,
skips the menacing flame
or water's gag
calmed when my heartbeat
slows to memory's speed.

Auschwitz and Dachau still
hover on the horizon.
Children still run in silence
through Guatemala's dense forests
and trudge hungry
across the parched Sudan.
Then time projects another scene.

Not all are sewn with terror's stitch.
A five-year-old's birthday
crowds minutes

that cannot age
on a map of perfect homes
their neat yards blooming
in my eyes.

It's all now, now, now,
as inventory crumbles
and is reborn.
I await some future algorithm
to reverse direction
surprise my words
and heal their tender baby flesh.

Nowhere and Everywhere

for those taken in South America's Dirty Wars

We lost and so we are not heroes.
If we had won
our names would be etched
on grateful granite,
parents would tell their children
bedtime stories
where we pull off feats
we never accomplished when we lived.
Streets would speak our names.

Our own children grew up
reinventing their lives,
some in the homes
of those who murdered their parents
and spirited them to a realm
where the dreams we died for
hide in moldy corners
biding clandestine time.
We are nowhere and everywhere.

We outlive the air we breathed
while weavers of history
pay us too much attention or none.
Schoolbooks, if they mention us at all,
treat us as warning.

If we had won
barracks would be playgrounds,
work plentiful and safe,
the sky a healthy blue.

Some Were Children

They kept coming. The building's crosscut interior
allowed me to see myself
running from window to balcony
pushing them out and off.
I watched them crash against the pavement below
only to rise again: no blood, no broken limbs,
returning like boomerangs.

Some were children. I thought I might feel
a pang as I heard them fall and hit,
but they rebounded to where I kept trying
to thrust them from me, destroy them definitively.
It was never enough and I could not win
this struggle that showed no evidence
of victory on either side.

Waking from the dream did nothing to end
our ominous dance. We are locked
in each other's claim on righteousness.
Every attacker, young or old,
has been sentenced to keep on fighting,
void of feeling and trying to reclaim the power
of every story we have ever known.

Long Leash

*"As for Pakal's dates, his birth, accession, and death
are attached to dates millions of years into the past
and thousands of years into the future—if you want to
move his dates around, you have to move
all of those dates as a body."*
—Linda Schele

Twelve hundred years ago
a queen at Tikal
looked into her obsidian mirror
and was haunted by the pain
I feel each morning
as I think of our Court's only Black judge
bloodying, with a stroke of his pen,
his people surging across the bridge
at Selma, or daring to vote
when the punishment was death.
The sun has us on a long leash.

Galileo rode the telescope
carrying him to the heavens.
Lenin lifted his ponderous forehead
and received the impact
of a bullet in nun's habit.
Popes bless multitudes,
their fingers sparkling with gems
that drip the blood
of South African miners

whose children are born hungry
and die of hunger
in the dawning of the light.

This week those Black Robes said
some of us can go ahead and marry,
we whose scarlet letter fades
on foreheads held in pride.
A State's blessing
like Mary Magdalene at the tomb,
or those tiny birds,
after saffron-robed monks
open their wooden cages.
They tremble briefly
before flying away.

When the young revolutionary
predicted a free people
would dream in Technicolor
he couldn't imagine
this roller coaster of ghosts.
At Sheep Springs,
young Aaron walks on Nike feet
that survived the march to Bosque Redondo
but were crushed
when he threw himself
beneath the tires of an 18-wheeler.

I cherish our love, yet know
it cannot light the path
of Sudan's wandering youth,

calm Syria's skies
or heal the lonely man
who pinned bits of color to his only shirt.
My arms bear the knowledge
of minutes,
my shape-shifter lineage
talks to his animal spirit
in cryptic dreams: a double helix
spiraling through this mystery called time.

Keeping My Body Politic Safe

One day my shadow turned a corner
as I walked straight ahead.
It tried not to look back
but turned
at the very last minute,
its sad eyes
hoping to bridge
the distance between us.

My shadow's lengthening stain
on wall or ground
showed more courage than I,
a stronger heart,
greater capacity for risk,
greater abandon
or less obedience
to the rules of the game.

Without my shadow I felt naked
and uncertain,
more vulnerable to heat and cold,
out of sync with my century.
Alone, I had to decide
whether arms are for swinging free
or covering up,
hands to create or excuse.

Forced to consider my shadow
separate from myself,
I remembered giving birth
then waving my children on their way,
holding to righteousness,
studying its face
and erasing the con artist's grin
while keeping my body politic safe.

In our time we've had to learn
to juggle PTSD,
closed-head injury and fewer limbs,
an eye for an eye
in endless wars of greed.
Forced to leave beloved countries,
exile's alchemy remains:
insurance against the shadow's loss.

Time Curls My Arthritic Toes

for my son Gregory

Buying a loaf of dark pumpernickel
from those aging brothers
at the Jewish bakery on 9th Street
my trusting twenty-something body
held no memory of future
but I was here to stay.

Voices whispered in my head
and new colors appeared
on the virgin sheet of paper
making its way through smoke
and food just starting to go bad.
You met me more than halfway.

Dawn broke on the Fulton Street Market
years before dumpster diving
found its way
into the Times Style Section.
Moving subway cars
rocked us to sleep.

As yesterday becomes tomorrow
today staggers to its feet,
turning its eyes to quiet.
Humiliation,

trailing such long history,
has nowhere to go but down.

Back then I couldn't yet see you, Son,
fighting your losing war
or building universities,
although I cradled you in arms
as hopeful as those
bringing home that dense dark bread.

Now time curls my arthritic toes
through long nights.
Landscape etches an underside of hope.
We wave goodbye to the leaders
who gathered us up, also remembering
those who later betrayed us.

My years are transparent membranes now
ripping sudden sound,
my bloom faithful to first insolent buds
as I peer back through the looking glass
at all those cracked promises:
Run Jane Run.

Unhinged Bodies Whisper

We build our lives over ancient graves
or on the rubble of buildings
whose shadowy walls leave us
juggling questions
lost between the lives they housed
and ours.

On the warm stones of *La plaza de tres culturas*
unhinged bodies whisper where they lay,
their flesh still brandishes
small glimmers of phosphorus,
words dense as jungles.

We know which culture won:
no denial of destiny when wind whistles
its layer of tangled dreams
and numbed travelers continue to search.
Memory rides a vast arc
but never settles far from home.

See her there with her basket of vegetables
hiding grenades and boxes of shells,
not those we find at the beach
or hold to our ear
hopeful for a symphony of waves.

Of course you don't. Her basket
has turned to dust,
centuries gone between her time and ours.
But careful where you step
with so many shards beneath your feet.

We inhabit this patchwork peopled by those
embarrassed for us:
every fishmonger finding himself
on desert dry as bone,
every child who cannot understand
why we do not answer when she calls.

Watch your step. Our lives unfold
in faltering symphony
over fields of hungry ghosts.

Cool Compresses and Nonbinding Law

Now the patient's fever spikes at dawn
as well as late afternoon.
Cool compresses and nonbinding law
do nothing to bring it down.

Glaciers melt, filling valleys with oceans of salt.
The patient must sleep upright.
Her lungs no longer expand
or retract in harmony.

Teeth chattering like insulted bone,
she sweats toxic waste
and fracking's poison,
vomits the bile of mutilated seed.

The fire on her brow swallows wilderness,
great cities and small towns.
Branches crackle like charred veins,
science fiction a pale portrait of her agony.

Preventative medicine was the only way
to avoid this fatal turn.
We're years past that now.
Breathtaking no longer means beautiful.

No morphine, hospice or final ritual, this illness
increases dangerous levels of testosterone.

The patient's fever rises off the charts,
her death a matter of time.

Her preventable disease reaches
every orphaned child, every pristine landscape
buried in ash, hurricane or earthquake
off the Richter scale.

A pandemic of rapes and murders opens
like sores on her once fertile body,
desperate migrations push
through permanently clogged arteries.

The patient's echoing warnings
may be observed or not
by some future species
when oblivious time returns.

Sifting Memory

Something happened here, or many somethings,
deliberate or laid at willing feet. Before me
others stood in this place, faced north
at just this time of day, crouched here,
walked through this sand, touched this rock.

I feel them breathing. My breath layers upon theirs,
fills the crevices between these sluices of earth,
rises in that roiling thunderhead at canyon's end.
What did they say? What words move
their centuries to mine?

Dream. Place. Image. Gift. It is all of these
until someone usurps it, proclaims it
a system with rules,
dresses it in subordination and control,
makes himself the priest.

Don't talk to me about Church. Don't impose
your greed of grandeur on experience
that survives all crass possession
while I am here, precisely here,
sifting memory through hungry fingers.

Where I Live and Die

I am in the picture frame but look
as if I want out.
The relative behind the shutter
must have commanded
come on now smile,
may have showed impatience
at my disinterest, refusal
to take my place in her tableaux.

Seventy years have passed. The image
is faded, its edges frayed
beyond their pinked irregularity
defining that home photography era.
I cannot remember what lay beyond
the picture plane,
what truth or action
social formality stole.

What I know is what I longed for then
without knowing its name
I have grabbed with both hands
and pulled onto this map
where I live and die
with all those
who invited me
into the inside looking in.

Horizon's Collarbone

From red earth glowing with Purple Sage
and Rabbit Brush,
Greasewood and Globe Mallow,
sandstone towers soar.

Sun descends between their silhouettes
and they pull shadowy blankets
about proud shoulders, past silent eyes
over their heads.

Horizon's collarbone keeps the broken wall
of a single-family dwelling safe.
Sinew and muscle, a sand-pitted skull
protects the ear of corn chewed clean.

Beneath the lightning crack where shale fell away
on this alcove's farthest wall
the artist left her mark: a bird's body and legs
crowned by antlers.

Night cancels day, then day returns
where female rain
erases the tiniest lizard track
and moon lets go its burden of shame.

These monoliths slumber shrouded in velvet
then throw their shadowy blankets off:

become incandescent again
making life possible.

This Poem's Got a Problem

This poem's got a problem,
an issue you might say
—mouthing linguistic dodge—
where vague carries the day
avoiding definition.

This poem wants to serve,
provoke chuckles
even outright laughter,
transmit the magic
of a charmed life.

But it slips from my grasp,
wanders under the railway bridge
where a family of seven
takes scant cover from the cold.
It notices hunger.

My poem takes an autumn walk
along the riverbank,
admires the gold-red turn
of Cottonwood leaves
until its morning calm

is split by the screams
of a woman forced
into the nearby woods:

some broken man
believes he has the right.

My poem tries to take refuge
in news or entertainment
(one and the same these days)
but today's school shooting
floods the screen.

On the other side of the world
27 members of a wedding party
are vaporized
because a novice recruit in Idaho
mistook them for enemy troops.

I am an optimist, light-hearted
and believe it or not
have a sense of humor,
but my poetry insists
on recording what it sees.

Your Poems Are So Political

Your poems are so political
the academy darling says,
implying deficiency
or some vague naiveté
as if I should know better at my age.

What moves me is the delicate membrane
where love's pulse
beats against submission,
subjugation erases will,
Big Guy versus everyone else.

Your gentle fingers braid mine
as we transit streets
where it's a crime
to love
outside the rules.

Shame as an acceptable place to be,
God with a capital G,
water wasted or poisoned
beneath a desert carved into greedy squares
crowding against my undulating bluffs.

Children who will never grow up,
who know there is nothing
to live for

but insist with a child's guile
they want to live.

War is never somewhere else, ravaging
a country of people I do not know
who look different
and whose words I cannot understand.
Every war ignites my fever.

Melting glaciers raise the level
of oceans
but also the bile rising from my gut.
When you know better you do better
seems to have lost its relevance.

Yes, I respond, *my poems*
are political like a razor
against your throat,
the word no when you expected yes,
spit in the eye of the powerful.

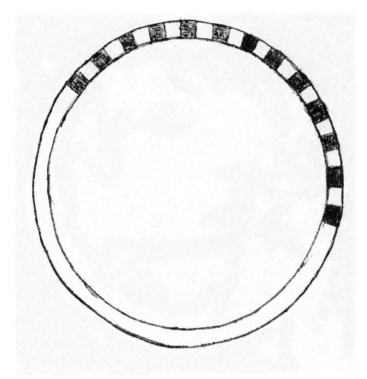

Notes

1. *Selva Vida,* by Stéfano Varese, Frédérique Apffel-Marglin, and Roger Rumrrill (Copenhagen, Denmark, Grupo Internacional de Trabajo Sobre Asuntos Indígenas; Mexico City, Mexico, Programa Universitario México Nación Multicultural; and Havana, Cuba, Fondo Editorial Casa de las Américas, 2013, p. 18).

2. *Muriel Rukeyser Reader,* edited by Jan Heller Levi (New York: W. W. Norton, 1994, p. 271).

3. Crazy Horse (ca. 1840 – September 5, 1877) was a warrior leader of the Oglala Lakota. He took up arms against the U.S. government to fight against encroachments on the territories and way of life of his people, including leading a war party to victory at the Battle of Little Big Horn in June 1876.

4. Harriet Tubman (born Araminta Harriet Ross, 1820 – March 10, 1913) was an African-American abolitionist and Union spy during the American Civil War. Born into slavery, she escaped and subsequently made more than nineteen missions to rescue more than 300 slaves using the network of anti-slavery activists and safe houses known as the Underground Railroad. She later helped recruit men for John Brown's raid on Harpers Ferry, and in the post-war era struggled for women's suffrage.

5. Thelonious Sphere Monk (October 10, 1917 – February 17, 1982) was an American jazz pianist and composer, considered one of the giants of American music.

6. Adrienne Cecile Rich (May 16, 1929 – March 27, 2012) was an American poet, essayist and feminist, one of the greatest poets of the twentieth century.

7. Popé (ca. 1630 – ca. 1688) was a Tewa leader from what has been known since the colonial period as San Juan Pueblo). He led the 1680 Pueblo Revolt against Spanish colonial rule. This was the first successful revolt against the Spanish. The Pueblo people expelled the colonists and kept them out of the territory for twelve years.

8. Adrienne Rich, see note 6.

9. Grace Paley (December 11, 1922 – August 22, 2007) was an American short story writer, poet, teacher, and political activist.

10. Anselm Paul Alexis Hollo (April 12, 1934 – January 29, 2013) was a Finnish poet and translator. He lived in the US from 1967 until his death in January 2013.

11. Gloria Evangelina Anzaldúa (September 26, 1942 – May 15, 2004) was a scholar of Chicana cultural theory, feminist theory, and queer theory.

12. Meridel Le Sueur (February 22, 1900 – November 14, 1996) was an American writer associated with the proletarian movement of the 1930s and 1940s.

13. James Mercer Langston Hughes (February 1, 1902 – May 22, 1967) was an African-American poet, social activist, novelist, playwright, and columnist.

14. Gwendolyn Elizabeth Brooks (June 7, 1917 – December 3, 2000) was an African-American poet. She won the Pulitzer Prize for Poetry in 1950.

15. Irwin Allen Ginsberg (June 3, 1926 – April 5, 1997) was an American poet and one of the leading figures of the Beat Generation of the 1950s and the decades until his death. In his epic poem "Howl," he denounced the destructive forces of capitalism and conformity in the United States.

16. Robert Creeley (May 21, 1926 – March 30, 2005) was an American poet, essayist and teacher. He is associated with the Black Mountain school of poetry.

17. Walter "Walt" Whitman (May 31, 1819 – March 26, 1892) was an American poet, essayist and journalist. His major work, Leaves of Grass, was criticized in its time for its overt homosexuality.

18. H.D. (born Hilda Doolittle; September 10, 1886 – September 27, 1961) was an American poet, novelist and memoirist known for her association with the early 20th century Imagist group.

19. Muriel Rukeyser (December 15, 1913 – February 12, 1980) was an American poet and political activist, best known for her poems about equality, feminism, social justice, and Judaism.

20. William Carlos Williams (September 17, 1883 – March 4, 1963) was an American poet closely associated with modernism and imagism. He was also a pediatrician and general practitioner of medicine.

21. King James version of the Bible, John 3:16.

22. From "Buffalo," *Winter Count*, Vintage, 1999.

23. Emmett Till was a 14-year-old Black boy from Chicago who in 1955 traveled with relatives to spend the summer in

Money, Mississippi. On August 24, he was accused of whistling at a white woman in a grocery store, and four days later was kidnapped, brutally beaten, murdered and his body weighted with 50 pounds of steel, bound with barbed wire and thrown into the Tallahatchie River. His murderers, Roy Bryant and J. W. Millam, were tried but acquitted by an all-white jury that took 67 minutes to produce its verdict. The two men freely admitted to, and boasted about, their crime, even selling their story to Look Magazine for $4,000; but because of double-jeopardy laws could not be retried. In 2012, Trayvon Martin was a 17-year-old high school student from Miami who was visiting his father in Sanford, Florida. In the early evening, during the halftime ceremonies of a game they were watching on TV, Trayvon went out to buy snacks. George Zimmerman, a neighborhood watch coordinator whose custom was to spot and harass people he felt were up to no good, saw him walking in his father's gated community. He called the police, who told him to stay in his car. Instead, he got out and followed the teenager on foot. When he caught up with him, they had words, and Zimmerman ended up shooting Martin at close range. He defended his action in the context of Florida's "Stand Your Ground" law, which allows any citizen to defend himself if he says he feels threatened by another. In July, 2013, Zimmerman went to trial. The state made sure the proceedings took place in a county controlled by extreme white racist Tea Party members. Race was not considered in the courtroom. It took an all-white jury of 6 women 16 hours to find Zimmerman not guilty, in a verdict that enraged defenders of justice throughout the nation.

Acknowledgments:

Some of these poems, occasionally in earlier versions, were first published in *Adobe Walls, Malpais Review, Mas Tequila Review, New Mexico Mercury,* and *The Ditchrider Sunday Poem* (New Mexico), *Cultural Weekly* (California), *Feminist Formations* (Arizona), *Prairie Schooner* (Nebraska), *Eyes Wide Open* (an anthology from West End Press, Albuquerque), and *Plaquetas bilingües* (Argentina).

About the Author

Margaret Randall is a feminist poet, writer, photographer and social activist. She is the author of over 100 books. Born in New York City in 1936, she has lived for extended periods in Albuquerque, New York, Seville, Mexico City, Havana, and Managua. Shorter stays in Peru and North Vietnam were also formative. In the 1960s with Sergio Mondragón, she co-founded and co-edited *El Corno Emplumado / The Plumed Horn*, a bilingual literary journal which for eight years published some of the most dynamic and meaningful writing of an era. From 1984 through 1994 she taught at a number of U.S. universities.

Randall was privileged to live among New York's abstract expressionists in the 1950s and early '60s, participate in the Mexican student movement of 1968, share important years of the Cuban revolution (1969-1980), the first four years of Nicaragua's Sandinista project (1980-1984), and visit North Vietnam during the heroic last months of the U.S. American war in that country (1974). Her four children—Gregory, Sarah, Ximena and Ana—have given her ten grandchildren. She has lived with her life companion, the painter and teacher Barbara Byers, for the past 27 years.

Upon her return to the United States from Nicaragua in 1984, Randall was ordered to be deported when the government invoked the 1952 McCarran-Walter Immigration and Nationality Act, judging opinions expressed in some of her books to be "against the good order and happiness of the United States." The Center for Constitutional Rights defended Randall, and many writers and others joined in an almost five-year battle for reinstatement of citizenship. She won her case in 1989.

In 1990 Randall was awarded the Lillian Hellman and Dashiell Hammett grant for writers victimized by political repression. In 2004 she was the first recipient of PEN New Mexico's Dorothy Doyle Lifetime Achievement Award for Writing and Human Rights Activism.

Recent non-fiction books by Randall include *To Change the World: My Life in Cuba* (Rutgers University Press), *More Than Things* (University of Nebraska Press), and *Che On My Mind* (Duke University Press). "The Unapologetic Life of Margaret Randall" is an hour-long documentary by Minneapolis filmmakers Lu Lippold and Pam Colby. It is distributed by Cinema Guild in New York City.

Randall's most recent collections of poetry and photographs are *Their Backs to the Sea* (2009) and *My Town: A Memoir of Albuquerque, New Mexico* (2010), *As If the Empty Chair: Poems for the disappeared / Como si la silla vacía: Poemas para los desaparecidos* (2011), *Where Do We Go From Here?* (2012), *Daughter of Lady Jaguar Shark* (2013) and *The Rhizome as a Field of Broken Bones* (2013), all published by Wings Press.

For more information about the author, visit her website at www.margaretrandall.org.

Wings Press was founded in 1975 by Joanie Whitebird and Joseph F. Lomax, both deceased. Bryce Milligan has been the publisher, editor and designer since 1995. The mission of Wings Press is to publish the finest in American writing—meaning all of the Americas—without commercial considerations clouding the choice to publish or not to publish.

Wings Press produces multicultural books, chapbooks, ebooks, and broadsides that, we hope, enlighten the human spirit and enliven the mind. Everyone ever associated with Wings has been or is a writer, and we know well that writing is a transformational art form capable of changing the world, primarily by allowing us to glimpse something of each other's souls. Good writing is innovative, insightful, and interesting. But most of all it is honest.

Likewise, Wings Press is committed to treating the planet itself as a partner. Thus the press uses soy and other vegetable-based inks, and as much recycled material as possible, from the paper on which the books are printed to the boxes in which they are shipped.

As Robert Dana wrote in *Against the Grain,* "Small press publishing is personal publishing. In essence, it's a matter of personal vision, personal taste and courage, and personal friendships." Welcome to our world.

Colophon

This first edition of *About Little Charlie
Lindbergh and other poems*, by Margaret
Randall, has been printed on 55 pound
EB "natural" paper containing a percent-
age of recycled fiber. Book titles have
been set in Papyrus type, the text in
Adobe Caslon Pro type. This book was
designed by Bryce Milligan.

On-line catalogue and ordering
available at
www.wingspress.com

Wings Press titles are distributed
to the trade by the
Independent Publishers Group
www.ipgbook.com
and in Europe by
www.gazellebookservices.co.uk

Also available as an ebook.